DARING TO STRUGGLE, FAILING TO WIN.

THE RED ARMY FACTION'S 1977 CAMPAIGN OF DESPERATION

BY J. SMITH & ANDRÉ MONCOURT

PM PRESS PAMPHLET SERIES

PM Press PAMPHLET SERIES No. 0002
DARING TO STRUGGLE, FAILING TO WIN:
THE RED ARMY FACTION'S 1977 CAMPAIGN OF DESPERATION
By J. Smith & André Moncourt
ISBN: 978-1-60486-028-3

PM Press
PO Box 23912
Oakland, CA 94623
www.pmpress.org

Kersplebedeb
CP 63560
CCCP Van Horne
Montreal, Quebec
Canada
H3W 3H8
http://www.kersplebedeb.com

http://www.germanguerilla.com

Layout and design: Courtney Utt

Printed in Oakland, CA on recycled paper with soy ink.

TABLE OF CONTENTS

INTRODUCTION

Thirty years ago, the world was a very different place.

The division between "Communism" and "The Free West"—détente notwithstanding—marked each and every political conflict, as did the anti-colonial revolutions, which had by no means run their course.

Millions of people around the world felt that it was reasonable and worthwhile to risk their lives fighting for liberation from capitalism and imperialism. Goals which were defined as such. This global upheaval found its epicentre in the Third World, and yet its effects would leave no nation untouched. While in the wealthy imperialist countries these liberation wars were most evident in the 1960s, there remained pockets of resistance, subcultural remnants, people who remained willing to put their lives on the line, fighting for revolution right through the 1970s and 1980s.

This pamphlet is one short sideways glance at a single chapter in this general twentieth century conflagration. It is a look at the most intense campaign waged by a group which no longer exists—the Red Army Faction—in a country which technically no longer exists—West Germany—at a point in history where "everything not busy being born, was busy dying." (with apologies to Bob Dylan).

The reasons for presenting this story are many.

First of all, those of us who are active on the left today operate within the same broad tradition as the people who risked and even lost their lives in 1977. If one cannot agree with all that the RAF did or said—to do so would mean closing our eyes to thirty years of history—one can still recognize them as comrades. So in a sense, telling this tale is a matter of showing respect.

Secondly, there are lessons here. They may not be obvious, the forms of struggle are so very different now than they were in the seventies, but there are things that can be learned nevertheless. Questions of how to wage asymmetrical warfare, of what we mean by revolutionary morality, of what we risk when we underestimate our opponents. Perhaps most importantly, the story of the RAF can teach us that it is possible to not back down, to surpass our previous expectations, to follow through on our most daring plans.

Unfortunately, many of the lessons to be learned from the RAF's struggle cannot be gleaned from 1977 alone. Interested readers are strongly advised to check out the upcoming two volume documentary history of the RAF that is to be published later this year by PM Press and Kersplebedeb. (For more on these volumes, see the contact pages at the end of this pamphlet.)

There is one more obvious reason for looking back at the RAF and the "German Autumn." This story has itself become politically relevant, as differing versions of what the RAF did and did not do, and what they did or did not think, have been imbued with symbolic importance for the new, 21st century, "united" Germany.

The year 2007 saw a glut of commemorations, ceremonies, and journalistic and scholarly retrospectives. Here the corpse of the RAF, and the memory of the dead on both sides, was put under a microscope as if we were assisting in an autopsy. Generally, the tone was excessively self-congratulatory: "we" beat the disease, "we" put it behind us. The "disease" in question being armed resistance to the imperialist state.

Mere memories can of course be tantalizing, and in certain quarters it was suggested that the "best" moments (from the point of view of the state, of course) could be relived: new charges against former combatants, new investigations into past assassinations, new repression against new radical movements too. More on this in the final section of this pamphlet.

Yet before we begin, a word is perhaps in order about the society in which all of this took place.

"West Germany," the Federal Republic of Germany, was an anti-communist state set up after World War II to threaten the Soviet bloc, and around which imperialism hoped to (and succeeded in) rebuilding the West European economy. As part of this process, immediately after the war the capitalist Allies decided to make peace with former Nazis and their supporters, so long as they were willing to play ball with the new "democratic" masters. Throughout the late 40s, the 50s, and the 60s, many of the key positions of power in the FRG were held by men who had played similarly important roles in Hitler's Third Reich.

As a substitute for any real denazification, religious and civil leaders simply repeated the mantra that the best way to make sure the crimes of the Nazi period would never happen again was for all Germans to concentrate on living "decent, law-abiding" lives. A message that would often be repeated by parents—not a few of whom had sieg heiling skeletons in their closets—to their children.

A stifling, authoritarian and conformist ideology was being imposed from above, a perfect match for the cultural wasteland that had been sterilized in the post-war period, just as it had been "aryanized" by fascism.

The wave of revolt that became known as the "New Left" reached the FRG at about the same time as it reached the other imperialist countries, in the 1960s. Gathered around Hans-Jürgen Krahl and the East German refugees Rudi Dutschke and Bernd Rabehl, in West Berlin some students began questioning not only the economic system, but the very nature of society itself. The structure of the family, the factory, and the school system were all challenged as these young rebels mixed the style of the hippie counter-culture with ideas drawn from the Frankfurt School's brand of Marxism.

Communes and housing associations began to spring up. Women challenged the male leadership and orientation within the SDS [Socialist German Student Union] and the APO [Extra-Parliamentary Opposition], setting up daycares, women's caucuses, women's centers, and women's only communes. The broader counterculture, rockers, artists, and members of the drug scene all rallied to the emerging political insurgency. Political protests encompassed traditional demonstrations, as well as sit-ins, teach-ins, and "happenings."

This revolt was all the more striking given the conservative cultural and political situation in West Germany at the time. Opposed by a rabidly right-wing gutter press and gratuitous police violence, the movement was forced to develop a capacity for street militancy, while the spectre of Germany's recent past imbued it with a sense of "do or die" urgency.

It was within this context, and inspired by the liberation struggles in the Third World, that the first militants began experimenting with a new form of political intervention: the urban guerilla.

SEVEN YEARS OF STRUGGLE AGAINST THE STATE

The Red Army Faction (RAF) had first announced itself in 1970, when a small group of radicals broke a young man out of jail.

Andreas Baader was serving a three-year sentence for having set a fire to a department store to protest the war in Vietnam. One of his rescuers, Gudrun Ensslin, had also participated in this political arson, and, as such, was also living underground at the time. Another rescuer, Ulrike Meinhof, was a well known left-wing social critic, a magazine journalist who had been finishing up a docudrama about girls in reform school. She was recognized and forced to go underground with the others.

The RAF made international headlines with this jailbreak, and the operation was hotly debated on the left.

Shortly thereafter, guerilla members travelled to Jordan, in the Middle East, where they received weapons training from the Palestinian group Al Fatah, part of the PLO. The RAF would make extensive use of various Arab countries as rear base areas throughout their existence, places where one could go not only for training, but also to hide when Europe got too "hot". As we shall see, this friendly relationship with Palestinian revolutionary organizations would have other consequences as well.

Upon their return to the FRG, the guerilla once again grabbed the public's attention, carrying out a series of bank robberies and preparing for campaigns to come.

Successfully evading police, the RAF began to take on the aura of folk heroes for many students and leftists who were glad to see someone taking things to the next level. Thousands of

May 1972: A car bomb goes off outside a police station in Augsburg.

people secretly carried photographs of RAF members in their wallets. Time and time again, as the cops stepped up their search, members of the young guerilla group would find doors open to them as they were welcomed into people's homes, including those of not a few middle class sympathisers academics, doctors, even a clergyman. Newspapers at the time carried stories under headlines like "Celebrities Protect Baader Gang" and "Sympathizers Hamper Hunt for Baader Group."

An opinion poll revealed that "40 percent of respondents described the RAF's violence as political, not criminal, in motive; 20 percent indicated that they could understand efforts to protect fugitives from capture; and 6 percent confessed that they were themselves willing to conceal a fugitive."[1]

Then, in May 1972, the group turned things up a notch, carrying out a series of bombings. Targets included police stations and U.S. army headquarters, to protest killer cops and the ongoing war in Vietnam. Four American soldiers were killed, and dozens of other people, including civilians, were injured. West Germany had never seen anything like it, and while many people may have been turned off by this escalation, others saw in these attacks an inspiring example of what could be done.

There followed a wave of repression as one hundred and thirty thousand cops, supported by both West German and U.S. intelligence units, set up checkpoints and carried out raids across the country.

Within a few weeks the leading members of the RAF—Andreas Baader, Gudrun Ensslin, Holger Meins, Jan-Carl Raspe and Ulrike Meinhof had all been captured. (It should be stressed: others were arrested too, and the RAF would always insist it had a non-hierarchical structure Nevertheless, the focus on these five is warranted for the purposes of this pamphlet, for these were the individuals the state considered key to the organization, and all five would die in prison, as will be detailed below.)

The state was not content to simply remove the perceived guerilla leadership from the field. Instead, it hoped to render them ineffective not only as combatants, but also as spokespeople for anti-imperialist resistance. To this end, it set up special "dead wings" in which political prisoners were subjected to severe isolation and sensory deprivation, with the clear hope that if this did not induce them recant, it might at least drive them insane.

....

1 Varon, Jeremy Bringing the War Home: The Weather Underground, the Red Army Faction, and Revolutionary Violence in the Sixties and Seventies, University of California Press 2004, p. 199.

Yet, captured and isolated, the guerilla managed not only to survive, but in a sense even turned things around. There were dozens of RAF members in prison, and dozens more political prisoners from other groups. Through the strategic use of hunger strikes these captured combatants

called attention not only to their conditions of incarceration, but also to their ideology of anti-imperialist armed struggle.

Prisoner support groups sprang up, and when Holger Meins died during a 1974 hunger strike, there were protests in cities across West Germany. The next day the 2nd of June Movement, a Berlin-based anarchist guerilla group, shot and killed the president of the West Berlin Supreme Court to avenge Meins and support the demands of the prisoners. Another judge had a bomb go off (harmlessly) outside his Hamburg residence, and there were eight firebombings in the university town of Gottingen.

Thousands met in university auditoriums in West Berlin to discuss possible responses, while thousands more braved the ban on demonstrations and took to the streets, battling police with stones and bottles. Protesters in Frankfurt and Mannheim smashed the windows of court buildings; even the Communist Party joined in, handing out fliers stating the obvious: "Holger Meins Murdered."[2]

Three thousand people attended Meins' funeral in Mannheim a week later, including Rudi Dutschke. The former sixties leader, standing over the grave as Meins' casket was lowered, famously gave the clenched fist salute, crying, "Holger, the fight goes on!"

The prisoners' struggle would serve to gain the RAF more than just supporters. It would also win new recruits, as in the eyes of many German leftists the RAF came to symbolize resistance to the imperialist state, to the "new fascism."

....
2 "Gunmen kill German judge", *Hagerstown Morning Herald*, November 11, 1974.

Following the death of Meins, the prisoners would continue their hunger strike until the regenerated RAF issued a communiqué addressed to them, in which it ordered them to start eating again. The guerilla promised that they would carry out the necessary actions on behalf of the prisoners, explaining that it would be "our weapons which will decide it.[3]

This would soon come to pass: on April 25, the RAF's "Holger Meins Commando" seized the top floor of the West German embassy in Stockholm, Sweden, taking twelve hostages. They demanded the release of twenty-six West German political prisoners, including Ensslin, Meinhof, Raspe, and Baader.

Swedish police rushed in, occupying the embassy's ground floor. They were repeatedly told to get out of the building, and the guerilla threatened to execute the FRG's Military Attaché if they did not do so. When the police failed to heed these warnings, Lieutenant Colonel Baron Andreas von Mirbach was shot through the head.

Seeing that the guerillas meant business, the police quickly vacated the premises, setting up their perimeter outside. A special intervention team was flown in from Hamburg, telephone lines to the embassy were cut, and the surrounding area was evacuated.

Under Chancellor Helmut Schmidt, the West German government refused to give in to the Commando's demands. For its part, the Swedish government tried to defuse the situation, offering them safe passage out of the country, but this was not acceptable: "It's useless, we're not negotiating," a guerilla spokesperson is said to have replied. "If our demands aren't met we shall shoot a hostage every hour. Victory or death!"

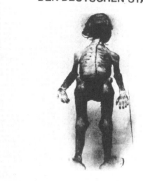

DIESER MANN ERPRESSTE

DEN DEUTSCHEN STAAT.

Holger Meins – im Hungerstreik am 7.11.1974 in der JVA Wittlich gestorben.

DEMONSTRATION   OPERNPLATZ

MITTWOCH 31.8. 16UHR

---

3 RAF *Communiqué to the prisoners, February 2nd 1975.*

Slightly more than one hour later, at 10:20 pm, the Commando shot dead Economic Attaché Heinz Hillegaart.

Shortly before midnight, as police were preparing to storm the building, the explosives the guerilla had laid detonated. The state and media would claim that the explosives went off due to some error on the part of the commando; the guerilla would suggest that the police intentionally triggered the explosion. One RAF member, Ulrich Wessel, was killed on the spot. Police rushed in, and RAF members Siegfried Hausner, Hanna Krabbe, Karl-Heinz Dellwo, Lutz Taufer, and Bernhard Rössner were all captured.

Despite the fact that he had a fractured skull and burns over most of his body, Hausner was only hospitalized for a few days. Then, despite

objections from doctors in Sweden and Germany, he was flown to Stammheim Prison where he died soon after.

The state had attempted to capitalize on its initial capture of the guerilla, only to find that from within prison they had managed to inspire their successors. Chancellor Helmut Schmidt

Government officials survey the damage the day after the Stockholm Occupation.

went so far as to state that "anarchist guerillas" now posed the greatest threat the Federal Republic had encountered during its twenty-six year history. Destroying the prisoners, or at least undercutting their support, became a top priority.

Fear mongering was stepped up; claims were made that the guerilla had nuclear weapons and was intent on kidnapping children to exchange for the prisoners. No claim was too preposterous, as those few who had broken were paraded out as state witnesses, alleging all kinds of horrors. Proof, or even mildly convincing evidence, was no longer deemed necessary.

Then on May 9, 1976, the state announced that Ulrike Meinhof had died in her cell, just as her trial was entering a critical phase. The authorities tried to spin a tale that Meinhof had committed suicide by hanging following a period of extreme depression provoked by tension between herself and her co-defendants, particularly between herself and Andreas Baader.

The prisoners, and most of the left, immediately denounced this as impossible, and did not hesitate to accuse the state of killing the woman who many viewed as the RAF's chief theoretician.

In Meinhof's own words, part of the court record the day before she was found dead, "It is, of course, a police tactic in counter-insurgency conflicts, in guerilla warfare, to take out the leaders."[4]

Meinhof's sister, Inge Wienke Zitzlaff, similarly rejected the state's version of events. "My sister once told me very clearly she never would commit suicide," she remembered. "She said if it ever were reported that she killed herself then I would know she had been murdered."[5]

"Freedom is possible only in the struggle for freedom." Poster commemorating the murder of Ulrike Meinhof, 1982.

An open letter signed by various intellectuals—including Jean-Paul Sartre and Simone de Beauvoir—compared Meinhof's death to the worst crimes of the Nazi era. Social and political prisoners in Berlin-Tegel Prison held a three-day hunger strike, and in Paris the offices of two West German steel companies were bombed, as was the German Cultural Center in Toulouse, and the German Academy and the West German Travel Bureau in Rome. Bombs went off in Munich outside the U.S. Armed Forces radio station and in a shopping center in the middle of the night. Thousands reacted with sorrow and rage, and demonstrations took place across West Germany.

Fighting was particularly fierce in Frankfurt; according to one police spokesperson, "the most brutal in the post-war history of the city." Following a rally, hundreds of people rampaged through the downtown area, breaking the windows at American Express and the America House cultural center, and setting up barricades and defending them against police water cannons with molotov cocktails. Twelve people were arrested

----

4 "Journalists Unearth Rare Terrorism Trial Tapes from 1970s," *Deutsche Welle*, July 31, 2007.
5 "Urban Guerilla Leader Hangs Herself in Cell" *The Hayward Daily Review* May 10 1976.

and seven cops were injured, two of them seriously when their car was set ablaze as they sat in it.

On May 15, some 7,000 people, many with their faces blackened and heads covered to avoid identification by the police, attended Meinhof's funeral in West Berlin. Wienke Zitzlaff requested that in lieu of flowers donations be made to the prisoners' support campaign, and when they left the cemetery mourners joined with demonstrations in downtown West Berlin and at the Moabit courthouse where Meinhof had been sentenced two years earlier in a previous trial.

That same day there were bomb attacks in Hamm in North Rhine-Westphalia, and also in Rome and Zurich. Three days later there was another demonstration of 8,000 people in West Berlin, during which

several police officers were injured. Bombs continued to go off in France, cars with German license plates and the offices of a right-wing newspaper being targeted. On June 2, the Revolutionary Cells bombed the U.S. Army Headquarters and U.S. Officers' Club in Frankfurt, carrying

Masked mourners gather at Meinhof's funeral

out the attack under the banner of the "Ulrike Meinhof Commando." That same day, just outside of the city, two fully loaded military trucks at a U.S. airbase were blown up.

An International Investigatory Commission into the Death of Ulrike Meinhof was formed; it took three years to release its findings, but in 1978 it claimed to have found evidence Meinhof had been brutally raped and murdered.

This then was the context in which the events of 1977 were to unfold. These were the guerilla and their supporters. This is what they had done. This is what the state had proven itself capable of.

But the story was far from over.

THE SUMMER OF 77: THE PRISONERS' STRUGGLE HEATS UP

By 1977, the Red Army Faction had managed to survive the arrests of its founding members five years earlier. Successfully countering isolation, psychological manipulation and sensory deprivation torture, the prisoners had in fact inspired their own successors, and through the strategic use of hunger strikes had come to symbolize resistance to the West German state and U.S. imperialism.

The prisoners' struggle was to remain central to the RAF throughout the decade, but at no point more so than in 1977.

On March 29 of that year, prisoners from the RAF and the anarchist 2nd of June Movement embarked upon their fourth hunger strike, demanding prisoner of war status, association in groups of no less than fifteen, an end to isolation, and an international investigation into the deaths of RAF prisoners in custody. Initially, thirty-five prisoners participated, but soon the number of prisoners refusing food surpassed one hundred and some prisoners escalated to refusing liquids.

The guerilla outside the prison walls was not going to let the prisoners wage this battle on their own. On April 7, as Attorney General Siegfried Buback was waiting at a traffic light in Karlsruhe, two individuals pulled up on a motorcycle alongside his Mercedes. Suddenly, one of them pulled out a submachine gun and fired, riddling the car with bullets.

As head of the Federal Prosecutor's Office, Buback bore direct responsibility for the prison conditions which had already claimed the lives of Ulrike Meinhof, Siegfried Hausner, and Holger Meins. It was in the name of the "Ulrike Meinhof Commando" that the RAF issued a communiqué claiming responsibility.

As has been noted elsewhere:

> This attack marked a shift to a strategy that would be marked
> by an overwhelming focus on assassinations of key members
> of the state apparatus and the business elite. Although this
> might not have been recognized at the time, it was a shift
> to an entirely new phase in the RAF's practice.[6]

Or, as one guerilla would later testify, the assassination "showed that we knew who they were, that we could attack them, and that there was nothing they could do to stop us."[7]

....
6 "A Brief History of the Red Army Faction," Arm the Spirit. From:
   http://www.hartford-hwp.com/archives/61/191.html
7 Knut Folkerts Statement in the Trial Against Brigitte Schulz and Christian
   Klar Regarding the Buback Assassination, June 5,1984.

Within a day police announced that Günter Sonnenberg, Knut Folkerts, and Christian Klar (formerly active in the prisoner support scene) were all sought in connection to the attack, a bounty of 200,000 marks ($88,000) being offered for their capture.

The hunger strike continued, the prisoners consolidating their support. Soon relatives of the prisoners began a solidarity strike, and on April 17, Peter's Church in Frankfurt was occupied and turned into a hunger strike information center. As the number of prisoners refusing food reached one hundred and twenty, more outside supporters began a second solidarity hunger strike in a Bielefeld Church. On April 27, relatives of political prisoners held a demonstration at the United Nations headquarters in Geneva demanding the application of the Geneva Convention. The next day, Amnesty International added its

Cop guards the body of former Attorney General Siegfried Buback

voice to that of eighty clergymen, one hundred and twenty-eight U.S. lawyers, one hundred French and Belgian lawyers and twenty-three English lawyers, all supporting the prisoners' demands.

Finally, on April 30, it was announced that the prisoners would be granted limited association. The seventh floor of Stammheim prison—where Baader, Raspe, and Ensslin were help along with RAF member Irmgard Möller—was soon being renovated to allow up to sixteen prisoners to be housed together. In response to this victory, the prisoners agreed to end their hunger strike.

On May 3, RAF members Günter Sonnenberg and Verena Becker were captured in the German-Swiss border town of Singen.

A woman had tipped off the police after spotting the two as they sat in a café: she recognized Sonnenberg from the wanted posters that had gone up throughout Western Europe after the Buback assassination.

When the police arrived on the scene the guerillas tried to play it cool, innocently pretending to have left their ID papers in their car. While being escorted from the café—presumably to retrieve these phantom ID papers—they drew their weapons and shot the two cops, commandeered a car and took off. Pursued by squad cars alerted to the incident, they took a wrong turn and ended up in a field, at which point they ditched their vehicle and tried to escape on foot.

As they fled, one of the guerillas dropped a submachine gun—as it would turn out, the same weapon that had been used to kill Buback. A cop picked the weapon up and fired: Becker was hit in her leg and Sonnenberg in his body and his head. His wounds were such that despite his being the object of such an intense manhunt it took several hours before he could be positively identified, and days later it was still unclear if he would survive.

As a result of his injuries, Sonnenberg suffered brain damage, and still to this day is prone to epileptic seizures.

The next attack occurred on July 30, as three RAF members, including Susanne Albrecht, came with flowers to the door of Jürgen Ponto, one of the most important businessmen in West Germany. Ponto had direct ties to many Third World governments and had served as an advisor to South Africa's brutal apartheid regime. He was also Albrecht's god-father. The guerilla attempted to abduct the businessman, but when he resisted they opened fire, shooting him five times. As Albrecht had been recognized by Ponto's wife, she signed her name to the guerilla's communiqué for this action.

(The political storm that ensued when it was learned that Ponto had never been warned by police that they knew his god-daughter was close to the RAF led the Federal Minister of the Interior Werner Maihofer to famously state that "There is no capitalist who does not have a terrorist in his own intimate circle of friends or relations.")

On August 8, the RAF prisoners who had been moved to Stammheim just a month earlier were transferred back to Hamburg. The precise excuse used was a "fight" with guards essentially a set up whereby the guards provoked an incident and used it as an excuse to attack and beat the prisoners. It appeared that Buback's replacement Kurt Rebmann had moved to reverse his previous decision to grant "association," the holding of political prisoners in common groups.

Baader, Raspe, Ensslin and Möller were once again alone on the seventh floor of Stammheim prison.

In reaction to these machinations and to the attack on Ponto, all RAF prisoners went on hunger strike, some escalating to a thirst strike almost immediately.

Within days force-feeding had begun a sadistic practice whereby prisoners were drugged, strapped down on a table, and had a pipe rammed down their throat for hours at a time. It was not meant to save the lives of the hunger strikers, but was another form of torture which the state had come to depend on in its struggle against the prisoners. Holger Meins, for instance, who had died during the 1974 hunger strike, had been force fed for weeks. As he wrote before his death:

> A red pipe, not a tube, is used, inserted in the stomach. The width of a finger; in my case, it is greased for ease of motion. This doesn't happen without provoking convulsive choking in the digestive tract, because the tube is only a millimeter or two narrower than the digestive tract. To avoid this it is necessary to make a swallowing motion and remain completely still. The slightest irritation when the pipe is introduced causes a vomiting reflex and the tensing up of the chest and stomach muscles; in a chain reaction these convulsions spread with violent intensity throughout the body. This causes one to buck against the pipe. The more difficult and violent this is, the more painful it is. The whole thing is nothing but torture, with vomiting accompanying the convulsions.[8]

Adelheid Schulz, a RAF member imprisoned in the 1980s, would describe the effects of force-feeding as "hours of nausea, a racing heartbeat, pain, and effects similar to fever. At times one experiences hot flashes; then one is freezing cold."[9]

Defence attorneys Armin Newerla and Arndt Müller began organizing public support for the striking prisoners and so came under heavy police surveillance. On August 15, the lawyers' offices were firebombed, almost certainly with the collusion of the police who had them staked out 24 hours a day. Newerla was subsequently arrested when copies of a left-wing magazine were found in his car and was charged with "supporting a criminal organization" under Paragraph 129. Seeing the writing on the wall, defence lawyer Klaus Croissant had already fled the country to France, where he requested political asylum.

The new Attorney General staked out the "hard-line" position that he would be remembered for. "I know that the population is not at all interested if these people go on hunger and thirst strikes," Rebmann

....
8 Meins, Holger *On Force Feeding*, 1974
9 *Von der Zwangernährung zur "Koma-Losung,"* West Germany, September 1985, p. 25.

told the press. "The population wants these people to be hit hard, just as hard as they have earned with their brutal deed."

He was asked about the possibility of prisoners dying. "That is always a bad thing," he answered, "but it would be the consequence which has been made clear to them and their lawyers and which is clear to them. The conditions of imprisonment don't justify such a strike; they are doing very well considering the circumstances."

On August 25, the RAF responded by targeting Rebmann's offices. An improvised rocket launcher was aimed at the Attorney General's headquarters, yet the timing device was not set properly, and so it failed to fire.

The RAF attempted to put this mishap in the best possible light, issuing a communiqué a week later in which they pretended that the entire exercise had merely been intended for show. The guerilla went out to warn that it was more than willing to act should it prove necessary to save the prisoners:

> Should Andreas, Gudrun, and Jan be killed, the apologists for the hard line will find out that they are not the only ones with an arsenal at their disposal. They will find out that we are many, and that we have enough love—as well as enough hate and imagination—to use both our weapons and their weapons against them, and that their pain will equal ours.[10]

The guerilla was clearly concerned, following Meinhof's murder, in the context of the hunger strikes and Rebmann's bloodthirsty statements that the state might move to kill Baader, Ensslin, and Raspe. This fear was shared by the prisoners themselves, who knew that they might suffer reprisals for the RAF's actions.

Indeed, fearing such reprisals, and following the breakdown of negotiations between Amnesty International and the Federal Government, on September 2, the prisoners called off their hunger and thirst strike. In a short statement, Jan-Carl Raspe explained that the attacks on Ponto and Rebmann had created an environment in which the prisoners had become hostages and the state was ready and willing to kill them to set an example.

....
10 RAF *Attack On The BAW Office in Karlsruhe*, September 3rd 1977.

GERMAN AUTUMN, BITTER DEFEAT

The failed Ponto kidnapping had been intended to be the first of a two-pronged action to put pressure on the West German ruling class to force the state to free the prisoners. Despite their failure to take Ponto alive, it was decided to follow through on the second part of this plan.

On September 5, the RAF's "Siegfried Hausner Commando" kidnapped Hanns-Martin Schleyer, the most powerful businessman in West Germany at the time. His car and police escort were forced to a stop by a baby stroller that was left out in the middle of the road, at which point they were ambushed by guerillas who killed his chauffeur, Heinz Marcisz, and three police officers—Reinhold Brändle, Helmut Ulmer, and Roland Pieler—before making their getaway.

A note received soon after warned that, "The federal government must take steps to assure that all aspects of the manhunt cease—or we will immediately shoot Schleyer without even engaging in negotiations for his freedom."[11]

Like Ponto, Schleyer was a frequent figure on television representing the ruling class point of view. He was the president of both the Bundesverband der Deutschen Industrie (Federal Association of German Industrialists)

Schleyer had joined the SS in 1933 just two months after his eighteenth birthday. A committed fascist, he held several important positions in the Nazi Student Association before and during the war. At the same time, in 1943, he began work for the Central Federation of Industry for Bohemia and Moravia where he was in charge of "Germanizing" the economy of Czechoslovakia. Following the Nazi defeat, he was captured by French forces and imprisoned for three years, classified as a "fellow traveller" by the denazification authorities. He was released in 1949 and used his experience during the Nazi occupation of Czechoslovakia to get a posting to the foreign trade desk in the Baden-Baden Chamber of Commerce and Industry. ("Schleyer, a German Story" by Heike Friesel October 2004 accessed at http://www.litrix.de/buecher/sachbuecher/jahr/2004/schleyer/enindex.htm on October 28 2007.

11 RAF *Schleyer Communiqué (first)*, September 5, 1977

and the Bundesvereinigung der Deutschen Arbeitgeberverbände (Federal Association of German Employers), and had earned a reputation for aggressively opposing workers' demands when he had ordered a lock-out of striking metal workers in Baden-Württemberg state in 1966. As a veteran of Hitler's SS, he was

Scene of devastation after Hans Martin Schleyer was seized, his driver and police escort killed.

a perfect symbol of the integration of former Nazis into the post-war power structure.

As the guerilla would later explain:

> *We hoped to confront the SPD [Social Democratic Party] with the decision of whether to exchange these two individuals who embody the global power of West German capital in a way that few others do.*
>
> *Ponto for his international financial policy (revealing how all the German banks, especially his own Dresdner Bank, work to support reactionary regimes in developing countries and also the role of West German financial policy as a tool to control European integration) and Schleyer for the national economic policy (the big trusts, corporatism, the FRG as an international model of social peace).*
>
> *They embodied the power within the state which the SPD must respect if it wishes to stay in power.*[12]

Despite the failure of the Ponto action, the RAF felt that the plan could not be called off, that lives were at stake: "the prisoners had reached a point where we could no longer put off an action to liberate them. The prisoners were on a thirst strike and Gudrun was dying.[13]

Within a day of Schleyer's kidnapping, the commando demanded the release of eleven prisoners including the RAF founders Gudrun Ensslin, Jan-Carl Raspe, and Andreas Baader and their safe passage to a country of their choice.

Despite the fact that the prisoners offered assurances that they would not return to West Germany or participate in future armed actions if

....
12 RAF *The Resistance, the Guerilla and the Anti-Imperialist Front*, May 1982.
13 Ibid.

exiled, on September 6, the state released a statement indicating that they would not release the prisoners under any circumstances.

On the same day, a total communication ban was instituted against all political prisoners. The so-called Kontaktsperre law, which had been rushed through parliament in a matter of days specifically to deal with this situation, deprived the prisoners of all contact with each other as well as with the outside world. All visits, including those of lawyers and family members, were forbidden. The prisoners were also denied all access to mail, newspapers, magazines, television, and radio.

In short, those subjected to this law were placed in 100% individual isolation.

On September 9, Agence France Presse's Bonn office received the first ultimatum from the commando holding Schleyer, setting a 1:00pm deadline for the release of the prisoners. The state countered with a proposal that Denis Payot, a well-known human rights lawyer based in Geneva, act as a go between. Secret negotiations began the same day.

On September 22, RAF member Knut Folkerts was arrested in Utrecht after a shoot-out which left one Dutch policeman dead and two more injured. He would eventually be convicted of Buback's murder. A woman, identified as RAF member Brigitte Mohnhaupt, managed to get away. The search for Schleyer was extended to Holland, but to no avail.

On September 30, defence attorney Ardnt Müller was arrested. Accused of having worked with his colleagues Armin Newerla and Klaus Croissant to recruit for the RAF, he was imprisoned under Kontaktsperre conditions. The arrest was buttressed by the claim that, on September 2, Müller had used Newerla's car, in which an incriminating map had allegedly been found. The next day, Croissant, who had fled to France earlier that year, would be arrested in Paris.

On October 7, the thirty-second day of the kidnapping, newspapers in France and Germany received a letter from Schleyer, accompanied by a photo, decrying the "indecisiveness" of the authorities.

On October 13, with negotiations deadlocked, a Palestinian commando intervened in solidarity with the RAF, putting the already intense confrontation on an entirely different level.

The four-person Commando Martyr Halimeh, led by Zohair Youssef Akache of a Popular Front for the Liberation of Palestine splinter group, Waddi Haddad's PFLP (External Operations), hijacked a Lufthansa airliner travelling from Majorca, Spain to Frankfurt in West Germany—ninety

people on board were taken hostage.

The airliner was first diverted to Rome to refuel and to issue the commando's demands. These were the release of the eleven RAF prisoners and two Palestinians being held in Turkey, Mahdi Muhammed and Hussein Muhammed al Rashid, who were serving life terms for a shootout at Istanbul airport in 1976 in which four people were killed.

The plane flew to Cyprus and from there to the Gulf where it landed first in Bahrain and then in Dubai.

It was now the morning of October 14. Denis Payot announced receipt of a communiqué setting a deadline of 8:00am on October 16 for all the demands to be met, "if a bloodbath was to be avoided." A videotape of Schleyer accompanied the communiqué, signed by both the Commando Martyr Halimeh and the Siegfried Hausner Commando.

Later that day, the West German government released a statement specifying that they intended to do everything possible to find "a reasonable and humanitarian solution" so as to save the lives of the hostages. That evening the Minister in Charge of Special Affairs, Hans Jürgen Wischnewski, left Bonn for Dubai.

On October 15, Payot announced that he had an "extremely important and urgent" message for the Siegfried Hausner Commando from the federal government in Bonn. Wischnewski, on site in Dubai, promised that there would be no military intervention. That evening, the West German media broke its self-imposed silence (which had been requested by the state) for the first time since the kidnapping, showing a thirty-second clip from the Schleyer video received the day before.

As another day drew to a close, the West German government announced that Somalia, South Yemen, and Vietnam had all refused to accept the RAF prisoners or the two Palestinians held in Turkey.

At eight o'clock in the morning on October 16, the forty-first day since the kidnapping of Schleyer, the deadline established in the October 14 ultimatum passed. In Geneva, Payot once again announced that he had received an "extremely important and urgent" message from Bonn. At 10:43am, the Turkish Minister of Finance and Defence declared that the Turkish government was prepared to release the two Palestinians should the West German government request it.

At 11:21am, the hijacked airliner left Dubai.

At noon, a second ultimatum passed.

At 3:20am on October 17, the hijacked airliner landed in Mogadishu, Somalia. The dead body of Flight Captain Jürgen Schumann, who had apparently sent out coded messages about the situation on board, was pushed out the door.

As the sun was rising the hijackers extended their deadline once again, and so it was at 2:00pm that yet another deadline passed. Minutes earlier a plane carrying Wischnewski and the GSG-9, a West German anti-terrorist commando, had landed in Mogidishu.

At the same time, in Germany Schleyer's family released a statement announcing their willingness to negotiate directly with the kidnappers.

That night, as the double-standoff continued, the government issued a statement that the "terrorists" had no option but to surrender. Less than an hour later, the West German government requested an international news blackout of developments at the airport in Mogidishu.

At 11:00pm on October 17, sixty members of the GSG-9 attacked the airliner; guerilla fighters Zohair Youssef Akache, Hind Alameh, and Nabil Harb were killed, and Souhaila Andrawes was gravely wounded.

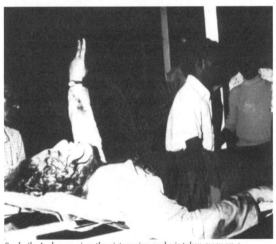

All hostages were rescued unharmed, with the exception of one man who suffered a heart attack.

The next morning, at 7am on October 18, a government spokesperson publicly announced the resolution of the hijacking.

An hour later, another spokesperson announced the "suicides" of Gudrun Ensslin and Andreas Baader and the

Souhaila Andrawes gives the victory sign as she is taken away on a stretcher: the three other members of her commando had been killed.

"attempted suicides" of Jan-Carl Raspe and Irmgard Möller. Raspe subsequently died of his wounds.

To all appearances, the prisoners had been killed in retaliation for the guerilla's actions. The RAF issued a communiqué announcing that it,

in turn, had executed Schleyer. On the evening of October 19, police recovered his body in the trunk of a car in the French border town of Mullhaus, just where the RAF had said it would be.

After forty-three days, the most intense clash between the anti-imperialist guerillas and the West German state had come to its bloody conclusion, sending shock waves through every sector of West German society.

The German Autumn affected the entire West German left, and the state responded to the '77 offensive with a wave of repression against the revolutionary movement.

On April 25, just a few weeks after the RAF had killed Siegfried Buback, a student newspaper had published an essay entitled Buback Obituary, in which the anonymous author admitted his "secret joy" at the Attorney General's assassina-

Gundrun Ensslin hung in her cell, and Andreas Baader shot through the back of the head; Jan-Carl Raspe (shown here alive) was also murdered in Stammheim prison.

tion. While the Buback Obituary was hostile to the RAF's politics, and in fact argued against armed struggle, the state seized upon the opportunity to clamp down on the radical left and sympathetic academics.

At the same time, the plethora of Maoist parties and pre-party formations which then existed in the FRG had also entered the state's sights. After Schleyer was seized, the state moved to ban the three largest Maoist parties, the KBW, the KPD, and the KPD/ML, with ludicrous claims that they had some connection to "terrorism". All three organizations called for a joint demonstration in Bonn on October 8, 1977, under the slogan "Marxism-Leninism Cannot Be Outlawed!" Twenty thousand people marched under red flags in what would be the only joint activity these sectarian organizations would mount during the decade.

Most of these Maoist groups would implode within a few years, losing many members to the new Green Party. Yet other militants managed to break through the impasse of '77 while affirming their radical politics, by organizing a radical left countercultural happening, Tunix, held in January 1978 in West Berlin. As the organizers ("Quinn the Eskimo", "Frankie Lee," and "Judas Priest") explained in their call out:

> When our identity is under attack, like during the situation in the fall of '77, then we need to take the initiative and state openly what it is we want. Political taboos and appeals to the constitution won't save us.[14]

The Tunix conference represented a breakthrough for the anti-authoritarian "sponti" scene, with as many as twenty thousand people attending. Participants took to the streets of West Berlin, throwing bricks and paint filled eggs at the courthouse, the America House, and the women's prison. Banners read: "Free the prisoners!" "Out With the Filth," and "Stammheim is Everywhere."

Nevertheless, this was a time of defeat and demoralization. As a later writer would note:

> While some people sought to criticize the state's violence (for example, 177 professors issued a statement), most people were simply left speechless by the events. Whole streets were lined with cops with machineguns, known left-wing radicals were stopped and searched, and radical left meeting places were raided.
>
> The 'German Autumn' forced the undogmatic radical left scene to re-orient itself away from factory struggles and squatting efforts and towards the growing anti-nuclear actions... In the context of the anti-imperialist attacks and hijackings by the RAF (and some barely identifiable Arab forces) during the '77-Offensive, the process of the splitting off of the radical left scene, which began in 1972, was complete. Increased state repression, coupled

....
14 Geronimo *Fire and Flames: A History of the German Autonomist Movement*, PM Press, forthcoming.

> *with denunciations and distancing by left-liberals and academics from the '68-generation, made the whole affair a traumatic experience for the radical left.*
>
> *During this phase of isolation and disorientation, many comrades lapsed into resignation or joined up with the alternative movement. Another wing 'hibernated' in the anti-nuclear movement for a while.*[15]

As the RAF would later acknowledge: "We committed errors in '77 and the offensive was turned into our most serious setback."[16]

It would take some time for the guerrilla to formulate the lessons to be drawn from this unprecedented setback, to regroup and to plan its next moves.

THE STAMMHEIM "SUICIDES"[17]

An examination of the contradictions surrounding the alleged "suicides" of Gudrun Ensslin, Jan-Carl Raspe, and Andreas Baader, contradictions no less numerous than in the case of Ulrike Meinhof's death, tends to support the conclusion that the deaths were in fact murders.

Baader and Raspe died as a result of gunshot wounds, Ensslin as a result of hanging, and the sole survivor, Irmgard Möller, suffered repeated stab wounds inflicted with a kitchen knife.

As the two men were alleged to have shot themselves, some explanation as to where the guns had come from was necessary. Remember: the four had all been kept in complete isolation since Schleyer had been taken hostage, and had been in prison under harsh conditions for years before that.

On October 27, a spokesperson for the administration at Stammheim offered the necessary explanation. He stated that it is "not out of the question… that one of prisoners' lawyers passed the contraband articles to a prisoner during a visit."

Yet, such a thing does seem in fact to be "out of the question," if not flatly impossible. Before entering the visiting area, lawyers had to empty

......

15 Ibid.

16 RAF, *The Resistance, the Guerilla, and the Anti-Imperialist Front*, May 1982.

17 In recent years some, including RAF prisoners of the first generation, have claimed to know of a suicide pact involving the prisoners and have claimed certain knowledge that the deaths were a suicide. Irmgard Möller, the sole RAF survivor of the day's violence continues to insist that there was no suicide pact and that the prisoners were murdered.

their pockets and give their jackets to an employee for verification; they were body searched physically and with a metal detector. Prisoners were strip searched and inspected and given a new set of clothes both when entering and when leaving visits with lawyers. Further, due to the Kontaktsperre, the lawyers had been unable to see their clients after September 6.

As regards Andreas Baader, a plethora of other irregularities are apparent. Baader is supposed to have shot himself in the base of the neck in such a way that the bullet exited his forehead. Repeated tests indicated that it is virtually impossible for an individual to position a gun against his or her own body in such a way. Equally curious, there were three bullet holes in the cell. One bullet lodged in the wall, one in the mattress, and the third, the cause of death, lodged in the floor. Are we to presume Baader missed himself twice? As well, Baader had powder burns from the recoil on his right hand. Baader, however, was left-handed, and would almost certainly have used his left hand to shoot himself. In the case of Raspe, no powder burns were found at all. Powder burns always occur when firing a weapon.

The gun smuggling theory relied very heavily on the testimony of Hans Joachim Dellwo, brother of RAF prisoner Karl-Heinz Dellwo, and Volker Speitel, the husband of RAF member Angelika Speitel. They had both been arrested on October 2, 1977 and charged with belonging to a criminal association.

Under police pressure, both men would later admit to acting as couriers for the guerilla, and testify that they were aware of lawyers smuggling items to the prisoners during the Stammheim trial which had ended in April 1977 specifically they eventually claimed that guns had been smuggled in. The scenario put forth by the state was that these guns were then hidden away in the walls of the cells as work was done renovating the seventh floor that summer.

Yet Speitel and Dellwo's testimony was tainted by the fact that they provided it in order to avoid lengthy stays behind bars. In exchange for these allegations, they each received reduced sentences and new identities. As a result of their testimony, two defence attorneys would be tried and convicted of weapon smuggling in 1979.

As well as conveniently explaining the deaths, the gun smuggling story served two further purposes. From that point on, all lawyers' visits with RAF prisoners were through a screen, a process which facilitated auditory surveillance, as well as depriving the prisoners of one of their last direct human contacts. Furthermore, the guards were permitted, from that point on, to look through lawyers' files "to prevent smuggling."

In the case of Gudrun Ensslin's "suicide" there were further contradictions. The chair she allegedly used to hang herself was too far away from her body to have been used and the cable supporting her body would not likely have tolerated the weight of a falling body. As had been the case with Ulrike Meinhof, the histamine test that would have established whether Ensslin was dead before she was hanged was never undertaken.

Der Stammheimtod

In search of an explanation for this mass suicide, the state suggested that the prisoners realized there was no hope for their liberation following the storming of the hijacked airliner in Mogidishu and consequently chose mass suicide rather than life imprisonment. This explanation raises two questions. How would the prisoners, given the Kontaktsperre, have known about these developments? And, further, how would they have organized a group suicide under such conditions?

On October 20, authorities claimed to have "discovered" a radio in Raspe's cell, a cell that he had only occupied since October 4. The state alleged that, using the wall sockets and tools stolen while the prison was being renovated, the prisoners constructed an elaborate communication system that allowed them to monitor the radio broadcasts and to communicate with each other.

This was only the first in a series of very useful "discoveries." On October 22, two hundred and seventy grams of explosives were "discovered" in the prisoners' wing. On November 12, a razor blade and three detonators were "found" in Baader's cell. Finally, on December 12, a gun and ammunition were "found" in a cell formerly occupied by another RAF prisoner. It is worth noting that the gun in question was a Colt .38, the model used by special police units.

While the details of what happened that night may never be known, and the state's story cannot be 100% disproven, even taken at face value all the state's claims do not point to "simple suicide": in the final analysis their own evidence suggests that if prisoners would have had access to guns and radios then someone in a position of authority must have known it. Author Stefan Aust, for instance, suggests that the prisoners may have been allowed to believe they had established a "secret" communication system so that what they said to each other could be monitored. What emerges then is a picture of the prisoners being allowed to have weapons and being allowed to communicate with each other, and authorities listening in as a suicide pact was agreed upon and then acted on, all the while doing nothing to interfere.[18]

Yet one of the biggest problems with the suicide story, even in this form, is the fact that not all of the prisoners had died.

On October 27, Irmgard Möller, the only survivor from the alleged group suicide attempt, issued a statement claiming that she had NOT attempted suicide. She said that the last thing she heard before going to sleep on the night in question was two muffled explosive sounds. She was not aware of anything until she awoke some hours later feeling intoxicated and disoriented and having difficulty concentrating. She further stated that the prisoners had no contact with one another except by shouting through the air vents in their cells or when going by each other's cells on the way to or from the yard. Finally, she said the prisoners had absolutely no idea of developments in Mogadishu.

To this day, she maintains that the prisoners were murdered.

It is difficult to dispute such a claim, coming as it does from a woman who survived these events.

The prisoners had anticipated the possibility of murders disguised as suicides. On October 7 Andreas Baader sent his lawyer the following letter:

> *As a result of the measures of the last 6 weeks and a few remarks from the guards, one can draw the conclusion that the Administration of State Security, which—as a guard who is now permanently on the 7th floor has said— hopes to provoke one or more suicides here, or, in any case, create the plausible appearance of such. In this regard, I stress: None of us—this is clear from the few words that*

----

18 In this regard see Stefan Aust's *The Baader-Meinhof Group*, The Bodley Head Ltd London 1987, p. 432, 482-3, 487-8, 496-7, 550-552. Regarding the possibility that police might have learned of guns in Stammheim from Volker Speitel as early as October 4; see page 484. It should be noted that although Aust claims to believe the prisoners committed suicide, he emphasizes that there remain serious inconsistencies in the official version of events, including evidence pointing to the possibility that Baader was shot by a gun with a silencer on it, which would mean that the murder weapon was removed after he was killed (547), and also that guards lied when they claimed Möller had lifted her sweater before allegedly stabbing herself (548), a "fact" which the state claimed proved suicide as an assassin would not have tried to spare the victim's clothing.

we have been able to exchange at the doors in the last few weeks and from the years of discussion—have the intention of killing ourselves. Should we—again a guard—"be found dead," we have been killed, as is the procedure, in keeping with the tradition of legal and political measures here.[19]

Gudrun Ensslin had also written to her lawyers stating:

I am afraid of being suicided in the same way as Ulrike. If there is no letter from me and I'm found dead; in this case it is an assassination.[20]

Furthermore, in conversation with two prison chaplains on the afternoon of October 17, Ensslin had explained that there were three sheets of paper kept in a file in her cell, containing important information. "They should be sent to the head of the Chancellery if they do away with me, or if I'm executed," she said. "Please would you see that they get there? I'm afraid that otherwise the Federal Prosecutor will suppress or destroy them."[21]

Needless to say, according to the official account, these three sheets of paper were never found.

Although no independent body was ever formed to investigate the Stammheim deaths, the commission investigating the death of Ulrike Meinhof was still sitting at the time. They had several interesting comments. They noted that on both nights, May 8-9, 1976 and October 17-18, 1977, an auxiliary was in charge of surveillance rather than the usual person. They also noted that in both incidents the autopsies posed similar problems.

Regarding the incriminating evidence "turned up" by prison authorities during the cell searches, they approvingly quoted from the press release of Irmgard Möller's lawyer, Jutta Bahr-Jendgen, of October 25, 1977:

Why these inventories of the cells without neutral witnesses, without lawyers, these inventories which have produced receivers, radios, Morse code apparatuses, quantities of plastic explosives might as well find atomic bombs?[22]

19 Aust, op. cit., p. 489.
20 *Libération (Special Issue), Paris* 1978, p. 27.
21 Aust op cit. p. 526.
22 *La Mort d'Ulrike Meinhof: Rapport de la Commission international d'enquête*, Librairie François Maspero, Paris, 1979, p. 67.

"Gundrun, Andreas and Jan were tortured and murdered at Stammheim prison.

ERMORDET

IN TOTALISOLATION UND KONTAKTSPERRE

"irmgard möller erklärt: es hat zwischen andreas, gudrun, jan und ihr zu keiner zeit eine absrade gemein samen suizids gegeben. sie hat keinen suizid unternommen. sie hat sich die vier stichwunden in ihrer linken brustseite nicht selbst beigebracht. ihre letzte wahrnehmung vor eintritt von bewußtlosigkeit waren zwei knallgeräusche und ein quietschendes geräusch. das war dienstag den 18.10.77 um ungefähr 4 uhr 30."

SOFORTIGE FREILASSUNG VON IRMGARD MÖLLER
ZUSAMMENLEGUNG VON MINDESTENS 15 POLITI=
SCHEN GEFANGEN IN INTERAKTIONSFÄHIGEN GRUPPEN
WIR UNTERSTÜTZEN EINE INTERNATIONALE KOMMISSION
ZUR AUFKLÄRUNG DER UMSTÄNDE UND DER
POLITISCHEN VERANTWORTLICHKEIT DER
MORDE UND MORDVERSUCHE IN STAMMEIM
WIR RUFEN AUF ZU EINEM

EUROPÄISCHEN AKTIONSTAG.10.12

The Commission further noted the existence of an uncontrolled entrance to the seventh floor, which opened into the cell area, and which was not visible from the guard's office. This entrance was not acknowledged by authorities until November 4, 1977. The Commission observes:

> *This indicates that—as citizens have been saying for some time—the functionaries of the BKA [Federal Criminal Bureau], the BND [Federal Intelligence Service], and the Secret Services have a constant, uncontrolled access to the cells.*[23]

The cover-up was so glaring that the Frankfurter Rundschau, wrote, in reference to the official investigation:

> *The Parliamentary Commission is faced with ... three sorts of witnesses: those who know nothing, those who don't want to know anything and those who aren't allowed to make a statement.*[24]

As a macabre postscript to all of this, RAF prisoner Ingrid Schubert was moved into isolation in Munich-Stadeheim prison on November 11, 1977. One hour later she was found hanged dead. As in the case of Meinhof and Ensslin, the autopsy failed to find the usual signs of death by hanging.[25]

On the Thursday before her death, she had assured her lawyer that she had no intention of committing suicide.

....

23 Ibid, pp. 55-58.
24 Ibid, p. 68.
25 *Libération*, op. cit, p. 43.

LOOKING BACK FROM A DIFFERENT WORLD

Over thirty years has passed since the RAF suffered this "greatest defeat."

It took almost two years after the events of October 1977 before the RAF could mount its next attack. During that time, many of the fighters who had carried out the '77 campaign were captured. Some were killed. Still others made themselves scarce, fleeing to the Middle East and from there to the German Democratic Republic—East Germany—where the "communist" secret service provided them with new identities. This would blow up in the guerilla's face years later when the East German regime crumbled and almost all of these veterans would eventually cooperate with the new unified German state, helping it to hunt down their former comrades. But that is another story, told in the second volume of our documentary history.

When the RAF did re-emerge, it once again included a core of guerilla veterans and a new generation of younger activists. These younger activists were often inspired by the continuing struggles of the political prisoners, as had been many of the recruits in the mid-seventies. At the same time the guerilla would draw unprecedented support from the militant sections of the peace, squatter, and anti-nuclear movements, in a marked departure from previous experience.

In the 1980s, this process of renewal would play itself out more than once, until eventually the state, empowered by the "end of communism" in 1989, felt confident enough to short-circuit the entire cycle by releasing some prisoners and granting limited association to others. The RAF would in turn declare a unilateral ceasefire in 1992, and then finally disband six years later, not without much bitterness and mutual recriminations between different prisoners and those members of the guerilla still at large. Through de-escalation, in fact, the state would score a success where its previous hardline strategies had failed.

As stated in the introduction, looking back on 1977, we find ourselves peering through the looking glass, to a world perhaps familiar, and yet strikingly different.

1977 was a year of brinksmanship, as the guerilla attempted to take things to as intense a level as possible, hoping to force the state to back down. If they had succeeded, it would have certainly constituted a breakthrough for the revolutionary movement not only in West Germany, but throughout Western Europe.

But they failed. While they were not happy about the fact, capitalism's most powerful men were willing to sacrifice one of their own. Indeed, it seems obvious today that they never had any intention of conceding to the guerilla's demands. While the RAF's original plan was to also kidnap Ponto, even if this had succeeded it is unlikely the final outcome would have been any different.

One might argue that this was a result of the RAF's own audacity. Had the kidnapping demanded something less than the release of all RAF prisoners, had the state been put in a position where it would seem callous or inflexible by not giving in, things might have turned out differently. Yet, by 1977, the media and the state had carefully conditioned public opinion to reject "giving in to terrorists," and so the ruling class risked little by responding so aggressively.

The lesson seems to be that under ordinary circumstances the "democratic" state and ruling class can afford to sacrifice its individual representatives. Indeed, it may be argued that it can ill afford not to if faced with the threat of an even greater political reversal if it concedes to its opponents' demands. This is an example of how, in military conflicts between such unequal forces, political considerations take on great importance.

The intense repression which descended on the left during September and October 1977 made it almost impossible for sympathizers to rally

die front
entsteht
als kämpfende
bewegung!

The Front emerges as a fighting movement.
Sticker created by pro-RAF militants, 1980s.

in support of the prisoners or the guerilla. The impressive mobilizations of the spring and summer could not be repeated come fall: the level of combat now surpassed their capacities. This is not a matter of saying the guerilla's actions were unpopular—that goes without saying, even regarding their successful actions—but rather that even the minority who did identify with the RAF found itself overtaken by the force of events.

Finally, the decision to enlist the aid of a Third World liberation movement must be viewed as a serious error. The PFLP had pioneered skyjackings in the late 1960s, and was rooted in a legitimate struggle in which neither combatants nor non-combatants could be shielded from violence. Without passing judgement one way or another, the decision to take a plane full of hostages at least seems on a scale suited to the struggle against the cruelties of imperialist rule. Furthermore, such actions were understood by at least part of the base of the Palestinian guerilla groups as constituting part of their own liberation struggle.

However, taking a plane full of people hostage in order to secure the release of First World revolutionaries was a different matter. As the RAF would admit five years later in its 1992 May Paper:

> It was the first time a commando from a liberation movement directly intervened in the confrontation here and made the metropolitan struggle their own… It was an error not to seek the solution in the metropole itself rather than using a young national state to intensify matters, because the decision should have been based on the balance of power here—because it concerned the prisoners, who embodied the struggle here, and because it was a question of isolating the FRG. In connection with an action in the metropole, the goal of which was polarization in the metropole and to split the people from the state, this tactic—hijacking an airplane—could only neutralize the attack because the people in the plane found themselves in the same situation, treated as objects, as the imperialist state always and in all ways places people, thereby destroying the goal of a revolutionary action.

These were serious errors, and it should be noted that nothing similar to the Schleyer kidnapping was ever again attempted by the RAF or any of the other West German guerilla groups. From this point on, there would be no kidnappings or hostage takings to demand the release of prisoners.

While such operations had met with some success in the earliest years of the decade, by 1977 they had clearly run their course, an indication of the fact that the enemy will eventually learn how to negate any new tactic.

Hard lessons cannot be drawn from faraway events, nor can they be mechanically lifted from one context to another. However, in reviewing the struggles and sacrifices that have been carried out within our revolutionary tradition, we learn something of what has been and what may come again. Hopefully, one can draw some strength and insight from these battles of the past.

A FINAL NOTE

Our story is history, the history of a guerilla group with its roots in a 1968 firebombing and a 1970 prison break. Although the RAF dissolved itself a decade ago, the story is not yet over. When the RAF disappeared into the sunset in 1998, it left behind a good many prisoners, a number of whom had already been imprisoned in brutal prison conditions for more than twenty years. Most of them were released in the late 90s and in the early years of the 21st century, and 2007 saw two high-profile releases.

On February 12, 2007, Brigitte Mohnhaupt was released. Mohnhaupt had been one of the earliest RAF members, having made the jump from the small anarchist-oriented guerllia group, the Tupamaros-Munich, to the RAF in 1971. She was first imprisoned in connection with RAF activities from June 9, 1972 until February 8, 1977. Upon her release, she immediately went back underground, assuming a central role in the events of 1977 described above. On November 11, 1982, Mohnhaupt was again arrested, in the company of fellow RAF member Adelheid Schultz, when the

Christian Klar and Grigitte Mohnhaupt, 1977.

two women were visiting an arms cache staked out by the GSG-9 in a wooded area outside of Frankfurt. Mohnhaupt's second tour of duty had occurred in what is arguably the bloodiest period in the RAF's history, and she was sentenced to 5 life sentences, with a minimum 24-year mandatory sentence. Mohnhaupt's February 7, 2007 release sparked intense controversy in Germany. As we shall see, the state was not yet finished with Mohnhaupt.

Eva Haule, who had gone underground in 1984, was arrested on August 2, 1986 in a Rüsselheim ice cream parlor in the company of two supporters, Chris Kluth and Luiti Hornstein. She was charged in connection with the RAF's December 18, 1984 failed attack against the NATO SHAPE School in Oberammergau, as well as with membership in a terrorist organization, robbery, and possession of false documents, and on June 28, 1988, she was sentenced to 15 years in prison. But before she reached her 2001 release date, the state brought fresh charges against her in connection with the RAF's much-debated August 8, 1985 murder of Edward Pimental, a US soldier stationed in Germany. Pimental was killed by a RAF commando so that his ID card could be used to gain access to the US Rein-Main Air Base to carry out a bombing attack. Haule was finally released on August 7, 2007.

Another long-term RAF prisoner, Christian Klar, whose mandatory parole date comes up in 2009, made a bid for freedom in 2007 by applying for Presidential clemency. Klar, who was involved in RAF support activities beginning in 1973, and was first identified by the state as a RAF member in connection with the RAF's 1977 offensive, was arrested on November 16, 1982 when, as had been the case for Mohnhaupt and Schulz, he was visiting a RAF arms cache staked out by the GSG-9. Tried along with Mohnhaupt, he was found guilty on 9 counts of murder and 11 counts of attempted murder in connection with every RAF action carried out between from 1977 and his arrest: a 1977 shootout at the Swiss border, the assassination of Siegfried Buback, the assassination of Jürgen Ponto, the failed rocket attack of the BAW [Federal Prosecutors Office] in Karlsruhe in 1977, the Schleyer kidnapping and execution, a bank robbery and shootout in Zurich in 1979, and the 1981 failed assassination attempt against US General Frederick J. Kroesen. He was sentenced to 6 times life plus 15 years.

On May 7, 2007, President Horst Köhler denied Klar's clemency petition, mentioning a statement Klar had sent to the Rosa Luxemburg Congress in West Berlin in January of that year. Köhler pointed to one sentence in particular, in which Klar said that the time had come to "complete the defeat of the plans of capitalism and to open the door to another future."[26] This would not be the last setback Klar would see that year.

Klar is not the only RAF prisoner who remains in prison. Birgit Hogefeld, a member of the RAF during its final fractious period was lured, along with fellow RAF member Wolfgang Grams, into a GSG-9 ambush in Bad Kleinen on June 27, 1993 by police infiltrator Klaus Steinmetz. A shootout ensued, and when the dust had settled, GSG-9 agent Michael Newrzella and Grams were dead and Hogefeld was under arrest. On November 5, 1996, Hogefeld received 3 life sentences with a mandatory minimum of 15 years in connection with the August 8,1985 murder of Edward Pimental and two deaths as a result of the bombing at the US Rhein-Main Air Base, a failed assassination attempt against Hans Tietmeyer, the former President of the Deutsche Bundesbank on September 20, 1988, and the RAF's final armed action, the March 27, 1993

---

26 "Politicians Say 'Incorrigible' Terrorist Should Stay in Jail," Spiegel-Online, February 27, 2007, accessed at http://www.spiegel.de/international/0,1518,468956,00.html.

bombing destruction of a prison under destruction in Weiterstadt (the conviction in connection with this bombing would later be overturned on appeal). Like Klar, Hogefeld appealed for Presidential clemency, and, as was the case with Klar, Köhler rejected her application.

(There is a certain irony in Klar and Hogefeld being the last remaining RAF prisoners. During the fractious debate that raged amongst RAF prisoners between the 1992 ceasefire and the 1998 dissolution of the organization, Klar acted as spokesman for the hard line, while Hogefeld was a leading proponent of de-escalation.)

Sadly, Klar and Hogefeld may not long remain the only former RAF members in prison. The April 7, 1977 murder of former Attorney General Siegfried Buback has drawn renewed interest. Although 4 RAF members, Christian Klar, Knut Folkerts (released in 1995), Günter Sonnenberg (released in 1992), and Brigitte Mohnhaupt were convicted in connection with this murder, two former RAF members have stepped forward to claim that three of four were not in fact involved. Peter-Jürgen Boock claims certain knowledge that the motorcycle that carried the shooter was driven by Sonnenberg and that the shooter was in fact Stefan Wisniewski (released in 1999). Former RAF member Verena Becker has also stepped forward to point the finger at Wisniewski as the shooter. In her case, however, the waters are further muddied by the fact that she began cooperating with the state following her 1977 conviction on 6 counts of attempted murder and by the fact that there are several pieces of evidence connecting her to the shooting; the machinegun used was found in her possession, as was a screwdriver from the motorcycle's set, and a strand of her hair was found in one of the motorcycle helmets worn by the shooters.[27] As regards Folkerts alleged involvement in the shooting, former RAF member Silke Maier-Witt stepped forward to say that she informed the BKA in 1980 that Folkerts was with her in Amsterdam on the day of the shooting.

Authorities were quick to respond, with Minister of the Interior Wolfgang Schäuble calling on the Verfassungsschutz [Literally, Guardians of the Constitution—the police body primarily responsible for gathering intelligence on the guerilla and the left] and the BKA to investigate the allegations and Attorney General Monika Harms announcing that the BAW would be opening a new investigation. On January 3 of this

....

27 "Germany Revisits RAF Terrorism Verdict," Spiegel-Online, April 23, 2007, accessed at http://www.spiegel.de/international/germany/0,1518,478928,00.html.

year, a BGH [Federal Supreme Court] decision ordered that Folkerts, Mohnhaupt, and Klar be held for 6 months in coercive detention[28] or until they share with the investigating authorities what they know about the assassination. Klar, who remains in prison, risks having his sentence lengthened, while, for the time being, Mohnhaupt and Folkerts remain at liberty while they prepare an appeal. The three have received some support from left-wing members of parliament and left-wing intellectuals, but criticism has come from some unlikely places as well. Former Minister of the Interior Gerhart Baum, condemned the decision in a strongly worded reaction, saying, "Federal Prosecutors have known of suspicious facts regarding Wisniewski for 25 years and did nothing, which makes this whole thing embarrassing."[29] Buback's son Michael, no friend of the RAF, was also quick to denounce the decision, saying, "I suspect that even the BAW is sceptical as to what coercive detention will achieve. One thing is that the value of statements from former terrorists has long been a source of scepticism. And if such statements are the result of the pressure of coercive detention, one must be even more sceptical."[30]

Finally, a few words about the RAF members left stranded by the organizations dissolution in 1998. The information available indicates that 5 members were still active and undetained at that time. They were Burkhard Garweg, Daniela Klette, Andrea Klump, Horst Meyer, and Ernst Volker Staub. Garweg, Klette, and Staub are believed to be the three individuals who robbed an armored car in Duisburg on July 20, 1999, making off with an estimated 1 million DM. The three have joined a handful of earlier members whose whereabouts have not to this day been ascertained. Andrea Klump and Horst Meyer were not, however, so fortunate. They were approached by police in Vienna on September 15, 1999, and in the ensuing gun battle, Horst Meyer was shot dead and Andrea Klump was arrested. Klump was never successfully connected to any RAF actions, although she was for a time a suspect in the November 30, 1989 assassination of German banker Alfred Herrhausen. The evidence against Klump was, however, insufficient, and that murder remains unsolved until this day. Klump did, however, confess to a 1984 attempted bombing of a

----

28 Under German law, coercive detention can only be applied once.
29 "Ex-Innenminister Baum findet Beugehaft für RAF-Terroristen peinlich," Spiegel-Online,
   January 3, 2008, accessed at http://www.spiegel.de/politik/deutschland/0,1518,526604,00.html.
30 "Beugehaft für Ex-RAF-Mitglieder angeordnet—Buback-Sohn skeptisch," Spiegel Online,
   January 3, 2008, accessed at http://www.spiegel.de/politik/deutschland/0,1518,526533,00.html.

discotheque in Rota, Spain popular with US servicemen. The action was derailed by the accidental arrival on the scene of a police patrol. Klump, Meyer, and unidentified associates escaped following an exchange of fire with the police. Klump's confession earned her a 9-year sentence. Klump was also charged in connection with the December 23, 1991 car bombing of a busload of Russian Jewish refugees travelling through Budapest on their way to Israel. She confessed to prior knowledge, but denied active participation. However, forensic evidence connected both her and Meyer to this action, believed to be the work of an obscure Palestinian guerilla group, and Klump received an additional 12-year sentence. Neither of these actions were RAF actions, and Klump is not generally treated as a RAF prisoner.

Meanwhile, German authorities continue to pursue a number of unsolved cases connected to the RAF, occasionally ordering former RAF members and associates to provide DNA samples. And the search continues for the former members still…

BIBLIOGRAPHY AND SOURCES

We have purposefully not included many footnotes in this pamphlet, as our intention here has been to introduce people to a piece of history most North American activists do not know about. As such, this pamphlet is not intended to be a scholarly resource or reference.

The outline of this text has been determined not only by the well documented chain of events in 1977, but also by various communiqués and statements from the Red Army Faction and its captured combatants. These are included in our documentary history, and will also eventually be available on the German Guerilla website at www.germanguerilla.com

This text has also relied heavily on newspaper reports from the 1970s, especially *European Stars and Stripes*, the U.S. military's newspaper for its own troops. It also draws on Stefan Aust's account the Red Army Faction story, as told in his book *The Baader-Meinhof Group*, published in London by The Bodley Head Ltd in 1987. While Aust's book provides a wealth of detail, it should also be noted that it suffers from a real bias, located not only in his own politics but also in his apparent desire to paint Meinhof as being somehow "led astray" by other members of the group, especially Andreas Baader. This perhaps bears some relation to the fact that Aust was friends with Meinhof before she joined the guerilla.

Everything touched upon in this pamphlet is dealt with at greater length in *The Red Army Faction, a documentary history, Volume 1: Projectiles for the People*, along with footnotes and scholarly references.

FORTHCOMING FROM PM PRESS AND KERSPLEBEDEB:
THE RED ARMY FACTION: A DOCUMENTARY HISTORY
VOLUME 1: PROJECTILES FOR THE PEOPLE
ISBN: 978-1-60486-029-0
600 pages
Edited by André Moncourt & J. Smith
Introductory texts by André Moncourt & J. Smith
Translations by André Moncourt & J. Smith

The first in a two-volume series, this is by far the most in-depth political history of the Red Army Faction ever made available in English.

Projectiles for the People starts its story in the days following World War II, showing how American imperialism worked hand in glove with the old pro-Nazi ruling class, shaping West Germany into an authoritarian anti-communist bulwark and launching pad for its aggression against Third World nations. The volume also recounts the opposition that emerged from intellectuals, communists, independent leftists, and then—explosively—the radical student movement and countercultural revolt of the 1960s.

It was from this revolt that the Red Army Faction emerged, an underground organization devoted to carrying out armed attacks within the Federal Republic of Germany, in the view of establishing a tradition of illegal, guerilla resistance to imperialism and state repression. Bringing together seasoned veterans of the sixties movement, through its bombs and manifestos the RAF confronted the state with opposition at a level many activists today might find difficult to imagine.

For the first time ever in English, this volume presents all of the manifestos and communiqués issued by the RAF between 1970 and 1977, from Andreas Baader's prison break, through the 1972 May Offensive and the 1974 hostage-taking in Stockholm, to the desperate, and tragic, events of the "German Autumn" of 77. The RAF's three main manifestos—*The Urban Guerilla Concept*, *Serve the People*, and *Black September*—are included, as are important interviews with *Spiegel* and *le Monde Diplomatique*, and a number of communiqués and court statements explaining their actions.

Providing the background information that readers will require to understand the context in which these events occurred, separate thematic sections deal with the 1976 murder of Ulrike Meinhof in prison, the 1977 Stammheim murders, the extensive use of psychological operations and false-flag attacks to discredit the guerilla, the state's use of sensory depri-vation torture and isolation wings, and the prisoners' resistance to this, through which they inspired their own supporters and others on the left to take the plunge into revolutionary action.

Drawing on both mainstream and movement sources, this book is intended as a contribution to the comrades of today—and to the comrades of tomorrow—both as testimony to those who struggled before and as an explanation as to how they saw the world, why they made the choices they made, and the price they were made to pay for having done so.

KER
SPL
EBE
DEB

Since 1998 **Kersplebedeb** has been an important source of radical literature and agit prop materials, with over five hundred button designs in English and French, as well as dozens of t-shirts and a challenging selection of revolutionary literature.

The project has a non-exclusive focus on anti-patriarchal and anti-imperialist politics, framed within an anti-capitalist perspective. A special priority is given to writings regarding armed struggle in the metropole, and the continuing struggles of political prisoners and prisoners of war.

CHECK IT OUT ON THE WEB, OR WRITE FOR A FREE CATALOG:
KERSPLEBEDEB
CP 63560, CCCP Van Horne, Montreal, Quebec, Canada, H3W 3H8
http://www.kersplebedeb.com | info@kersplebedeb.com

PM Press was founded in 2007 as an independent publisher with offices in the US and UK, and a veteran staff boasting a wealth of experience in print and online publishing. Operating our own printing press enables us to print and distribute short as well as large run projects, timely texts and out of print classics.

We seek to create radical and stimulating fiction and non-fiction books, pamphlets, t-shirts, visual and audio materials to entertain, educate and inspire you. We aim to distribute these through every available channel with every available technology. Whether that means you are seeing anarchist classics at our bookfair stalls, reading our latest vegan cookbook at the café over (your third) microbrew, downloading geeky fiction e-books, or digging new music and timely videos from our website.

PM Press is always on the lookout for talented and skilled volunteers, artists, activists and writers to work with. If you have a great idea for a project or can contribute in some way, please get in touch.

PM Press . PO Box 23912 . Oakland CA 94623
www.pmpress.org